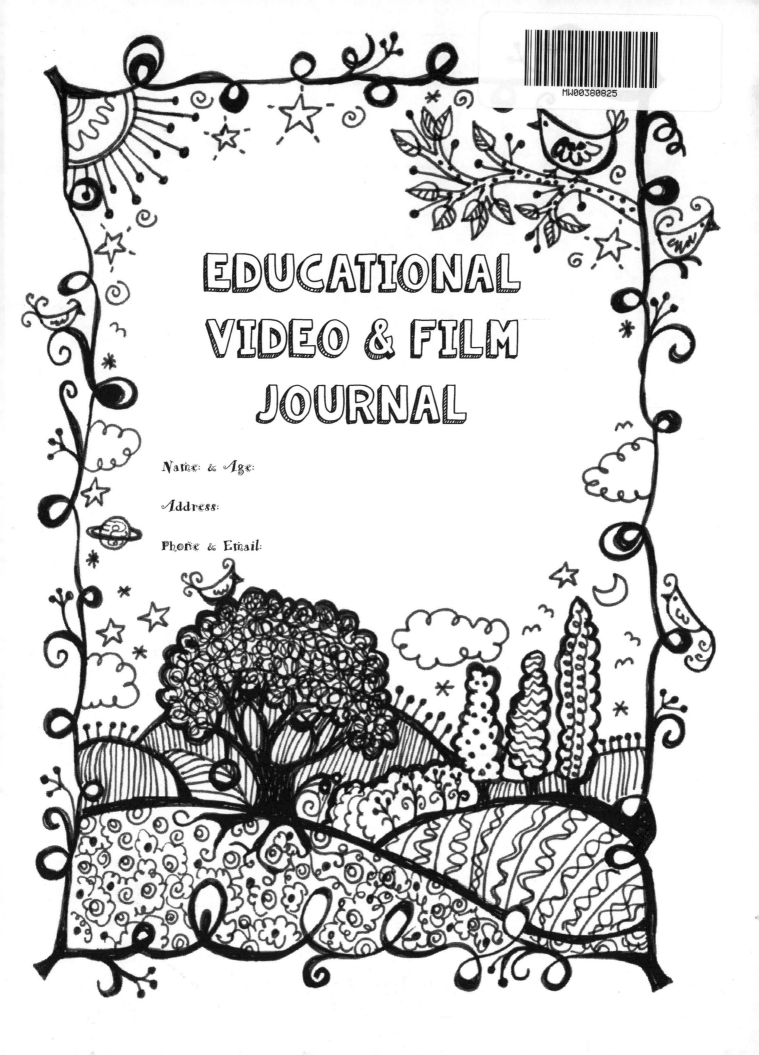

EDUCATIONAL VIDEO & FILM JOURNAL

Name: & Age:

Address:

Phone & Email:

TITLE:_____

Today's Date:_____

Producer:

_____

Actors:

_____

_____

_____

_____

_____

_____

_____

_____

_____

_____

Rating:

AWFUL

BAD

LAME

BORING

OKAY

NICE

GOOD

GREAT

SUPER

AMAZING

Draw a Scene from the video:

Notes:

TITLE:_____

Today's Date:_____

Producer:

_____

Actors:

_____

_____

_____

_____

_____

_____

_____

_____

_____

_____

Rating:
AWFUL
BAD
LAME
BORING
OKAY
NICE
GOOD
GREAT
SUPER
AMAZING

Draw a Scene from the video:

Notes:

TITLE:

TITLE:_____

Today's Date:_____

Producer:

_____

Actors:

_____

_____

_____

_____

_____

_____

_____

_____

_____

Rating:

AWFUL

BAD

LAME

BORING

OKAY

NICE

GOOD

GREAT

SUPER

AMAZING

Draw a Scene from the video:

Notes:

TITLE:_____

Today's Date:_____

Producer:

_____

Actors:

_____

_____

_____

_____

_____

_____

_____

_____

_____

_____

Rating:

AWFUL

BAD

LAME

BORING

OKAY

NICE

GOOD

GREAT

SUPER

AMAZING

Draw a Scene from the video:

Notes:

TITLE:_____

Today's Date:_____

Producer:

_____

Actors:

_____

_____

_____

_____

_____

_____

_____

_____

_____

Draw a Scene from the video:

Notes:

Rating:

AWFUL

BAD

LAME

BORING

OKAY

NICE

GOOD

GREAT

SUPER

AMAZING

Write a review about a film
that you watched this week:

TITLE:

_____

_____
_____
_____
_____
_____
_____
_____
_____
_____
_____
_____
_____
_____
_____
_____
_____

☆ ☆ ☆ ☆ ☆

Draw one of your favorite scenes or characters here.

Title:_____

Draw one of your favorite scenes or characters here.

Title:_____

TITLE:_____

Today's Date:_____

Producer:

_____

Actors:

_____

_____

_____

_____

_____

_____

_____

_____

_____

Rating:

AWFUL

BAD

LAME

BORING

OKAY

NICE

GOOD

GREAT

SUPER

AMAZING

Draw a Scene from the video:

Notes:

TITLE:

TITLE:_____

Today's Date:_____

Producer:

_____

Actors:

_____

_____

_____

_____

_____

_____

_____

_____

_____

_____

Rating:

AWFUL

BAD

LAME

BORING

OKAY

NICE

GOOD

GREAT

SUPER

AMAZING

Draw a Scene from the video:

Notes:

TITLE:

TITLE:_____

Today's Date:_____

Producer:

_____

Actors:

_____

_____

_____

_____

_____

_____

_____

_____

_____

Rating:

AWFUL

BAD

LAME

BORING

OKAY

NICE

GOOD

GREAT

SUPER

AMAZING

Draw a Scene from the video:

Notes:

Write a review about a film
that you watched this week:

TITLE:

_____

_____
_____
_____
_____
_____
_____
_____
_____
_____
_____
_____
_____
_____

☆ ☆ ☆ ☆ ☆

TITLE:_____

Today's Date:_____

Producer:

_____

Actors:

_____

_____

_____

_____

_____

_____

_____

_____

_____

Rating:

AWFUL

BAD

LAME

BORING

OKAY

NICE

GOOD

GREAT

SUPER

AMAZING

Draw a Scene from the video:

Notes:

TITLE:_____

Today's Date:_____

Producer:

_____

Actors:

_____

_____

_____

_____

_____

_____

_____

_____

_____

Rating:

AWFUL

BAD

LAME

BORING

OKAY

NICE

GOOD

GREAT

SUPER

AMAZING

Draw a Scene from the video:

Notes:

Draw one of your favorite scenes or characters here.

Title:_____

Draw one of your favorite scenes or characters here.

Title:_____

TITLE:_____

Today's Date:_____

Producer:

_____

Actors:

_____

_____

_____

_____

_____

_____

_____

_____

_____

_____

Draw a Scene from the video:

Notes:

Rating:

AWFUL

BAD

LAME

BORING

OKAY

NICE

GOOD

GREAT

SUPER

AMAZING

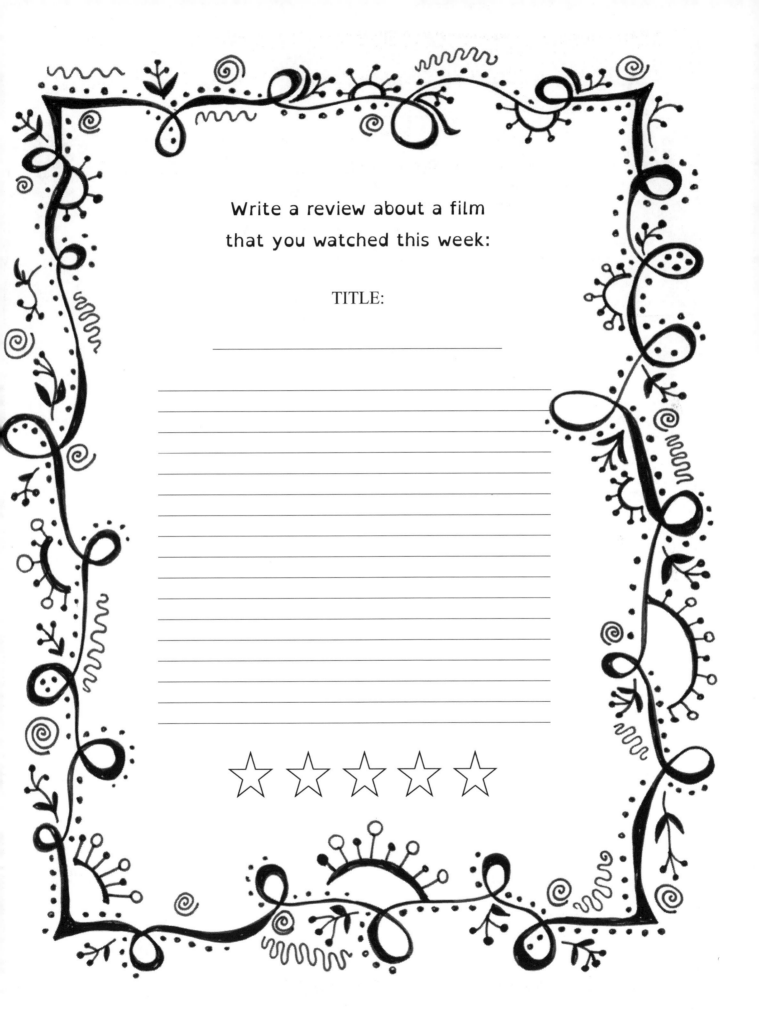

Write a review about a film
that you watched this week:

TITLE:

_____

TITLE:_____

Today's Date:_____

Producer:

_____

Actors:

_____

_____

_____

_____

_____

_____

_____

_____

_____

Rating:

AWFUL

BAD

LAME

BORING

OKAY

NICE

GOOD

GREAT

SUPER

AMAZING

Draw a Scene from the video:

Notes:

TITLE:_____

Today's Date:_____

Producer:

_____

Actors:

_____

_____

_____

_____

_____
_____
_____
_____
_____

Rating:

AWFUL

BAD

LAME

BORING

OKAY

NICE

GOOD

GREAT

SUPER

AMAZING

Draw a Scene from the video:

Notes:

TITLE:_____

Today's Date:_____

Producer:

_____

Actors:

_____

_____

_____

_____

_____
_____
_____
_____
_____

Rating:

AWFUL

BAD

LAME

BORING

OKAY

NICE

GOOD

GREAT

SUPER

AMAZING

Draw a Scene from the video:

Notes:

Write a review about a film
that you watched this week:

TITLE:

_____

_____
_____
_____
_____
_____
_____
_____
_____
_____
_____
_____
_____
_____
_____

☆ ☆ ☆ ☆ ☆

Draw one of your favorite scenes or characters here.

Title:_____

Draw one of your favorite scenes or characters here.

Title:_____

TITLE:_____

Today's Date:_____

Producer:

_____

Actors:

_____

_____

_____

_____

_____

_____

_____

_____

_____

Draw a Scene from the video:

Notes:

Rating:

AWFUL

BAD

LAME

BORING

OKAY

NICE

GOOD

GREAT

SUPER

AMAZING

TITLE:_____

Today's Date:_____

Producer:

_____

Actors:

_____

_____

_____

_____

_____

_____
_____
_____
_____
_____

Rating:

AWFUL

BAD

LAME

BORING

OKAY

NICE

GOOD

GREAT

SUPER

AMAZING

Draw a Scene from the video:

Notes:

TITLE:_____

Today's Date:_____

Producer:

_____

Actors:

_____

_____

_____

_____

_____

_____

_____

_____

_____

Draw a Scene from the video:

Notes:

Rating:

AWFUL

BAD

LAME

BORING

OKAY

NICE

GOOD

GREAT

SUPER

AMAZING

TITLE:_____

Today's Date:_____

Producer:

_____

Actors:

_____

_____

_____

_____

_____
_____
_____
_____
_____

Rating:

AWFUL

BAD

LAME

BORING

OKAY

NICE

GOOD

GREAT

SUPER

AMAZING

Draw a Scene from the video:

Notes:

TITLE:_____

Today's Date:_____

Producer:

_____

Actors:

_____

_____

_____

_____

_____

_____

_____

_____

_____

Rating:

AWFUL

BAD

LAME

BORING

OKAY

NICE

GOOD

GREAT

SUPER

AMAZING

Draw a Scene from the video:

Notes:

Write a review about a film
that you watched this week:

TITLE:

_____

_____
_____
_____
_____
_____
_____
_____
_____
_____
_____
_____
_____
_____

☆ ☆ ☆ ☆ ☆

Draw one of your favorite scenes or characters here.

Title:_____

Draw one of your favorite scenes or characters here.

Title:_____

TITLE:_____

Today's Date:_____

Producer:

_____

Actors:

_____

_____

_____

_____

_____
_____
_____
_____
_____

Rating:

AWFUL

BAD

LAME

BORING

OKAY

NICE

GOOD

GREAT

SUPER

AMAZING

Draw a Scene from the video:

Notes:

TITLE:_____

Today's Date:_____

Producer:

_____

Actors:

_____

_____

_____

_____

_____

_____

_____

_____

_____

Rating:

AWFUL

BAD

LAME

BORING

OKAY

NICE

GOOD

GREAT

SUPER

AMAZING

Draw a Scene from the video:

Notes:

TITLE:_____

Today's Date:_____

Producer:

_____

Actors:

_____

_____

_____

_____

_____

_____

_____

_____

_____

Draw a Scene from the video:

Notes:

Rating:

AWFUL

BAD

LAME

BORING

OKAY

NICE

GOOD

GREAT

SUPER

AMAZING

TITLE:_____

Today's Date:_____

Producer:

_____

Actors:

_____

_____

_____

_____

_____

_____

_____

_____

_____

Rating:

AWFUL

BAD

LAME

BORING

OKAY

NICE

GOOD

GREAT

SUPER

AMAZING

Draw a Scene from the video:

Notes:

TITLE:_____

Today's Date:_____

Producer:

_____

Actors:

_____

_____

_____

_____

_____
_____
_____
_____
_____

Rating:

AWFUL

BAD

LAME

BORING

OKAY

NICE

GOOD

GREAT

SUPER

AMAZING

Draw a Scene from the video:

Notes:

Write a review about a film
that you watched this week:

TITLE:

_____

_____
_____
_____
_____
_____
_____
_____
_____
_____
_____
_____
_____
_____
_____
_____

☆ ☆ ☆ ☆ ☆

Draw one of your favorite scenes or characters here.

Title:_____

Draw one of your favorite scenes or characters here.

Title:_____

TITLE:_____

Today's Date:_____

Producer:

_____

Actors:

_____

_____

_____

_____

_____

_____

_____

_____

_____

Draw a Scene from the video:

Notes:

Rating:

AWFUL

BAD

LAME

BORING

OKAY

NICE

GOOD

GREAT

SUPER

AMAZING

TITLE:_____

Today's Date:_____

Producer:

_____

Actors:

_____

_____

_____

_____

_____

_____

_____

_____

_____

Rating:
AWFUL
BAD
LAME
BORING
OKAY
NICE
GOOD
GREAT
SUPER
AMAZING

Draw a Scene from the video:

Notes:

TITLE:_____

Today's Date:_____

Producer:

_____

Actors:

_____

_____

_____

_____

_____

_____

_____

_____

_____

Rating:

AWFUL

BAD

LAME

BORING

OKAY

NICE

GOOD

GREAT

SUPER

AMAZING

Draw a Scene from the video:

Notes:

Write a review about a film
that you watched this week:

TITLE:

_____

_____
_____
_____
_____
_____
_____
_____
_____
_____
_____
_____
_____

☆ ☆ ☆ ☆ ☆

Draw one of your favorite scenes or characters here.

Title:_____

Draw one of your favorite scenes or characters here.

Title:_____

TITLE:_____

Today's Date:_____

Producer:

_____

Actors:

_____

_____

_____

_____

_____

_____

_____

_____

_____

Rating:

AWFUL

BAD

LAME

BORING

OKAY

NICE

GOOD

GREAT

SUPER

AMAZING

Draw a Scene from the video:

Notes:

TITLE:_____

Today's Date:_____

Producer:

_____

Actors:

_____

_____

_____

_____

_____

_____

_____

_____

_____

Rating:

AWFUL

BAD

LAME

BORING

OKAY

NICE

GOOD

GREAT

SUPER

AMAZING

Draw a Scene from the video:

Notes:

TITLE:_____

Today's Date:_____

Producer:

_____

Actors:

_____

_____

_____

_____

_____

_____

_____

_____

_____

_____

Rating:

AWFUL

BAD

LAME

BORING

OKAY

NICE

GOOD

GREAT

SUPER

AMAZING

Draw a Scene from the video:

Notes:

TITLE:_____

Today's Date:_____

Producer:

_____

Actors:

_____

_____

_____

_____

_____

_____

_____

_____

_____

_____

Draw a Scene from the video:

Notes:

Rating:

AWFUL

BAD

LAME

BORING

OKAY

NICE

GOOD

GREAT

SUPER

AMAZING

TITLE:_____

Today's Date:_____

Producer:

_____

Actors:

_____

_____

_____

_____

_____
_____
_____
_____
_____

Draw a Scene from the video:

Notes:

Rating:

AWFUL

BAD

LAME

BORING

OKAY

NICE

GOOD

GREAT

SUPER

AMAZING

Write a review about a film
that you watched this week:

TITLE:

_____

_____
_____
_____
_____
_____
_____
_____
_____
_____
_____
_____
_____
_____
_____

☆ ☆ ☆ ☆ ☆

Draw one of your favorite scenes or characters here.

Title:_____

Draw one of your favorite scenes or characters here.

Title:_____

TITLE:_____

Today's Date:_____

Producer:

_____

Actors:

_____

_____

_____

_____

_____

_____

_____

_____

_____

Draw a Scene from the video:

Notes:

Rating:
AWFUL
BAD
LAME
BORING
OKAY
NICE
GOOD
GREAT
SUPER
AMAZING

TITLE:_____

Today's Date:_____

Producer:

_____

Actors:

_____

_____

_____

_____

_____

_____

_____

_____

Rating:

AWFUL

BAD

LAME

BORING

OKAY

NICE

GOOD

GREAT

SUPER

AMAZING

Draw a Scene from the video:

Notes:

TITLE:_____

Today's Date:_____

Producer:

_____

Actors:

_____

_____

_____

_____

_____
_____
_____
_____
_____

Rating:
AWFUL
BAD
LAME
BORING
OKAY
NICE
GOOD
GREAT
SUPER
AMAZING

Draw a Scene from the video:

Notes:

Write a review about a film
that you watched this week:

TITLE:

_____

_____
_____
_____
_____
_____
_____
_____
_____
_____
_____
_____
_____
_____
_____

☆ ☆ ☆ ☆ ☆

TITLE:_____

Today's Date:_____

Producer:

_____

Actors:

_____

_____

_____

_____

_____
_____
_____
_____
_____

Rating:

AWFUL

BAD

LAME

BORING

OKAY

NICE

GOOD

GREAT

SUPER

AMAZING

Draw a Scene from the video:

Notes:

TITLE:_____

Today's Date:_____

Producer:

_____

Actors:

_____

_____

_____

_____

_____

_____

_____

_____

_____

_____

Rating:
AWFUL
BAD
LAME
BORING
OKAY
NICE
GOOD
GREAT
SUPER
AMAZING

Draw a Scene from the video:

Notes:

Draw one of your favorite scenes or characters here.

Title:_____

Draw one of your favorite scenes or characters here.

Title:_____

TITLE:_____

Today's Date:_____

Producer:

_____

Actors:

_____

_____

_____

_____

_____
_____
_____
_____
_____

Rating:

AWFUL

BAD

LAME

BORING

OKAY

NICE

GOOD

GREAT

SUPER

AMAZING

Draw a Scene from the video:

Notes:

Write a review about a film
that you watched this week:

TITLE:

_____

_____
_____
_____
_____
_____
_____
_____
_____
_____
_____
_____
_____
_____

☆ ☆ ☆ ☆ ☆

TITLE:_____

Today's Date:_____

Producer:

_____

Actors:

_____

_____

_____

_____

_____

_____

_____

_____

_____

Rating:
AWFUL
BAD
LAME
BORING
OKAY
NICE
GOOD
GREAT
SUPER
AMAZING

Draw a Scene from the video:

Notes:

TITLE:_____

Today's Date:_____

Producer:

_____

Actors:

_____

_____

_____

_____

_____

_____

_____

_____

_____

Rating:

AWFUL

BAD

LAME

BORING

OKAY

NICE

GOOD

GREAT

SUPER

AMAZING

Draw a Scene from the video:

Notes:

TITLE:_____

Today's Date:_____

Producer:

_____

Actors:

_____

_____

_____

_____

_____

_____

_____

_____

_____

Rating:

AWFUL

BAD

LAME

BORING

OKAY

NICE

GOOD

GREAT

SUPER

AMAZING

Draw a Scene from the video:

Notes:

Write a review about a film
that you watched this week:

TITLE:

_____

_____
_____
_____
_____
_____
_____
_____
_____
_____
_____
_____
_____
_____

☆ ☆ ☆ ☆ ☆

Draw one of your favorite scenes or characters here.

Title:_____

Draw one of your favorite scenes or characters here.

Title:_____

TITLE:_____

Today's Date:_____

Producer:

_____

Actors:

_____
_____
_____
_____

_____
_____
_____
_____
_____

Draw a Scene from the video:

Notes:

Rating:
AWFUL
BAD
LAME
BORING
OKAY
NICE
GOOD
GREAT
SUPER
AMAZING

TITLE:_____

Today's Date:_____

Producer:

_____

Actors:

_____

_____

_____

_____

_____

_____

_____

_____

_____

_____

Rating:

AWFUL

BAD

LAME

BORING

OKAY

NICE

GOOD

GREAT

SUPER

AMAZING

Draw a Scene from the video:

Notes:

TITLE:_____

Today's Date:_____

Producer:

_____

Actors:

_____

_____

_____

_____

_____
_____
_____
_____
_____

Rating:
AWFUL
BAD
LAME
BORING
OKAY
NICE
GOOD
GREAT
SUPER
AMAZING

Draw a Scene from the video:

Notes:

TITLE:_____

Today's Date:_____

Producer:

_____

Actors:

_____

_____

_____

_____

_____

_____

_____

_____

_____

_____

Rating:

AWFUL

BAD

LAME

BORING

OKAY

NICE

GOOD

GREAT

SUPER

AMAZING

Draw a Scene from the video:

Notes:

TITLE:

TITLE:_____

Today's Date:_____

Producer:

_____

Actors:

_____

_____

_____

_____

_____

_____

_____

_____

_____

Rating:

AWFUL

BAD

LAME

BORING

OKAY

NICE

GOOD

GREAT

SUPER

AMAZING

Draw a Scene from the video:

Notes:

Write a review about a film
that you watched this week:

TITLE:

_____

_____
_____
_____
_____
_____
_____
_____
_____
_____
_____
_____
_____

☆ ☆ ☆ ☆ ☆

Draw one of your favorite scenes or characters here.

Title:_____

Draw one of your favorite scenes or characters here.

Title:_____

TITLE:_____

Today's Date:_____

Producer:

_____

Actors:

_____

_____

_____

_____

_____

_____

_____

_____

_____

_____

Rating:

AWFUL

BAD

LAME

BORING

OKAY

NICE

GOOD

GREAT

SUPER

AMAZING

Draw a Scene from the video:

Notes:

TITLE:_____

Today's Date:_____

Producer:

_____

Actors:

_____

_____

_____

_____

_____

_____

_____

_____

_____

_____

Rating:
AWFUL
BAD
LAME
BORING
OKAY
NICE
GOOD
GREAT
SUPER
AMAZING

Draw a Scene from the video:

Notes:

TITLE:

TITLE:_____

Today's Date:_____

Producer:

_____

Actors:

_____

_____

_____

_____

_____

_____

_____

_____

_____

Rating:

AWFUL

BAD

LAME

BORING

OKAY

NICE

GOOD

GREAT

SUPER

AMAZING

Draw a Scene from the video:

Notes:

TITLE:_____

Today's Date:_____

Producer:

_____

Actors:

_____

_____

_____

_____

_____

_____

_____

_____

_____

Rating:
AWFUL
BAD
LAME
BORING
OKAY
NICE
GOOD
GREAT
SUPER
AMAZING

Draw a Scene from the video:

Notes:

TITLE:_____

Today's Date:_____

Producer:

_____

Actors:

_____

_____

_____

_____

_____

_____

_____

_____

_____

_____

Rating:

AWFUL

BAD

LAME

BORING

OKAY

NICE

GOOD

GREAT

SUPER

AMAZING

Draw a Scene from the video:

Notes:

Write a review about a film
that you watched this week:

TITLE:

_____

_____
_____
_____
_____
_____
_____
_____
_____
_____
_____
_____
_____
_____
_____
_____

☆ ☆ ☆ ☆ ☆

Draw one of your favorite scenes or characters here.

Title:_____

Draw one of your favorite scenes or characters here.

Title:_____

TITLE:_____

Today's Date:_____

Producer:

_____

Actors:

_____

_____

_____

_____

_____

_____

_____

_____

_____

_____

Draw a Scene from the video:

Notes:

Rating:
AWFUL
BAD
LAME
BORING
OKAY
NICE
GOOD
GREAT
SUPER
AMAZING

TITLE:_____

Today's Date:_____

Producer:

_____

Actors:

_____

_____

_____

_____

_____

_____

_____

_____

_____

Rating:

AWFUL

BAD

LAME

BORING

OKAY

NICE

GOOD

GREAT

SUPER

AMAZING

Draw a Scene from the video:

Notes:

TITLE:_____

Today's Date:_____

Producer:

_____

Actors:

_____

_____

_____

_____

_____

_____

_____

_____

_____

Rating:

AWFUL

BAD

LAME

BORING

OKAY

NICE

GOOD

GREAT

SUPER

AMAZING

Draw a Scene from the video:

Notes:

Write a review about a film
that you watched this week:

TITLE:

_____

_____
_____
_____
_____
_____
_____
_____
_____
_____
_____
_____
_____
_____

☆ ☆ ☆ ☆ ☆

Draw one of your favorite scenes or characters here.

Title:_____

Draw one of your favorite scenes or characters here.

Title:_____

TITLE:_____

Today's Date:_____

Producer:

_____

Actors:

_____

_____

_____

_____

_____

_____

_____

_____

_____

Rating:

AWFUL

BAD

LAME

BORING

OKAY

NICE

GOOD

GREAT

SUPER

AMAZING

Draw a Scene from the video:

Notes:

TITLE:_____

Today's Date:_____

Producer:

_____

Actors:

_____

_____

_____

_____

_____

_____

_____

_____

_____

_____

Rating:

AWFUL

BAD

LAME

BORING

OKAY

NICE

GOOD

GREAT

SUPER

AMAZING

Draw a Scene from the video:

Notes:

TITLE:_____

Today's Date:_____

Producer:

_____

Actors:

_____

_____

_____

_____

_____
_____
_____
_____
_____

Rating:

AWFUL

BAD

LAME

BORING

OKAY

NICE

GOOD

GREAT

SUPER

AMAZING

Draw a Scene from the video:

Notes:

TITLE:_____

Today's Date:_____

Producer:

_____

Actors:

_____

_____

_____

_____

_____

_____

_____

_____

_____

Rating:

AWFUL

BAD

LAME

BORING

OKAY

NICE

GOOD

GREAT

SUPER

AMAZING

Draw a Scene from the video:

Notes:

TITLE:_____

Today's Date:_____

Producer:

_____

Actors:

_____

_____

_____

_____

_____

_____
_____
_____
_____
_____

Rating:

AWFUL

BAD

LAME

BORING

OKAY

NICE

GOOD

GREAT

SUPER

AMAZING

Draw a Scene from the video:

Notes:

Write a review about a film
that you watched this week:

TITLE:

_____

_____
_____
_____
_____
_____
_____
_____
_____
_____
_____
_____
_____
_____
_____
_____

☆ ☆ ☆ ☆ ☆

Draw one of your favorite scenes or characters here.

Title:_____

Draw one of your favorite scenes or characters here.

Title:_____

TITLE:_____

Today's Date:_____

Producer:

_____

Actors:

_____

_____

_____

_____

_____
_____
_____
_____
_____

Rating:

AWFUL

BAD

LAME

BORING

OKAY

NICE

GOOD

GREAT

SUPER

AMAZING

Draw a Scene from the video:

Notes:

TITLE:_____

Today's Date:_____

Producer:

_____

Actors:

_____

_____

_____

_____

_____
_____
_____
_____
_____

Rating:

AWFUL

BAD

LAME

BORING

OKAY

NICE

GOOD

GREAT

SUPER

AMAZING

Draw a Scene from the video:

Notes:

TITLE:_____

Today's Date:_____

Producer:

_____

Actors:

_____

_____

_____

_____

_____

_____

_____

_____

_____

Draw a Scene from the video:

Notes:

Rating:
AWFUL
BAD
LAME
BORING
OKAY
NICE
GOOD
GREAT
SUPER
AMAZING

Write a review about a film
that you watched this week:

TITLE:

_____

_____
_____
_____
_____
_____
_____
_____
_____
_____
_____
_____
_____
_____

☆ ☆ ☆ ☆ ☆

TITLE:_____

Today's Date:_____

Producer:

_____

Actors:

_____

_____

_____

_____

_____

_____

_____

_____

_____

Rating:
AWFUL
BAD
LAME
BORING
OKAY
NICE
GOOD
GREAT
SUPER
AMAZING

Draw a Scene from the video:

Notes:

TITLE:_____

Today's Date:_____

Producer:

_____

Actors:

_____

_____

_____

_____

_____

_____

_____

_____

_____

_____

Rating:

AWFUL

BAD

LAME

BORING

OKAY

NICE

GOOD

GREAT

SUPER

AMAZING

Draw a Scene from the video:

Notes:

Draw one of your favorite scenes or characters here.

Title:_____

Draw one of your favorite scenes or characters here.

Title:_____

TITLE:_____

Today's Date:_____

Producer:

_____

Actors:

_____

_____

_____

_____

_____

_____

_____

_____

_____

Rating:

AWFUL

BAD

LAME

BORING

OKAY

NICE

GOOD

GREAT

SUPER

AMAZING

Draw a Scene from the video:

Notes:

Write a review about a film
that you watched this week:

TITLE:

_____

_____
_____
_____
_____
_____
_____
_____
_____
_____
_____
_____
_____
_____

☆ ☆ ☆ ☆ ☆

TITLE:_____

Today's Date:_____

Producer:

_____

Actors:

_____

_____

_____

_____

Rating:

AWFUL

BAD

LAME

BORING

OKAY

NICE

GOOD

GREAT

SUPER

AMAZING

Draw a Scene from the video:

Notes:

TITLE:_____

Today's Date:_____

Producer:

_____

Actors:

_____

_____

_____

_____

_____

_____

_____

_____

_____

Rating:

AWFUL

BAD

LAME

BORING

OKAY

NICE

GOOD

GREAT

SUPER

AMAZING

Draw a Scene from the video:

Notes:

TITLE:_____

Today's Date:_____

Producer:

_____

Actors:

_____

_____

_____

_____

_____

_____

_____

_____

_____

Rating:
AWFUL
BAD
LAME
BORING
OKAY
NICE
GOOD
GREAT
SUPER
AMAZING

Draw a Scene from the video:

Notes:

Write a review about a film
that you watched this week:

TITLE:

_____

_____
_____
_____
_____
_____
_____
_____
_____
_____
_____
_____

☆ ☆ ☆ ☆ ☆

Draw one of your favorite scenes or characters here.

Title:_____

Draw one of your favorite scenes or characters here.

Title:_____

TITLE:_____

Today's Date:_____

Producer:

_____

Actors:

_____

_____

_____

_____

_____

_____

_____

_____

_____

_____

Draw a Scene from the video:

Notes:

Rating:

AWFUL

BAD

LAME

BORING

OKAY

NICE

GOOD

GREAT

SUPER

AMAZING

TITLE:_____

Today's Date:_____

Producer:

_____

Actors:

_____

_____

_____

_____

_____

_____

_____

_____

_____

Rating:

AWFUL

BAD

LAME

BORING

OKAY

NICE

GOOD

GREAT

SUPER

AMAZING

Draw a Scene from the video:

Notes:

TITLE:_____

Today's Date:_____

Producer:

_____

Actors:

_____

_____

_____

_____

_____

_____

_____

_____

_____

Rating:
AWFUL
BAD
LAME
BORING
OKAY
NICE
GOOD
GREAT
SUPER
AMAZING

Draw a Scene from the video:

Notes:

TITLE:_____

Today's Date:_____

Producer:

_____

Actors:

_____

_____

_____

_____

_____

_____

_____

_____

_____

Rating:

AWFUL

BAD

LAME

BORING

OKAY

NICE

GOOD

GREAT

SUPER

AMAZING

Draw a Scene from the video:

Notes:

TITLE:_____

Today's Date:_____

Producer:

_____

Actors:

_____

_____

_____

_____

_____

_____

_____

_____

_____

Rating:

AWFUL

BAD

LAME

BORING

OKAY

NICE

GOOD

GREAT

SUPER

AMAZING

Draw a Scene from the video:

Notes:

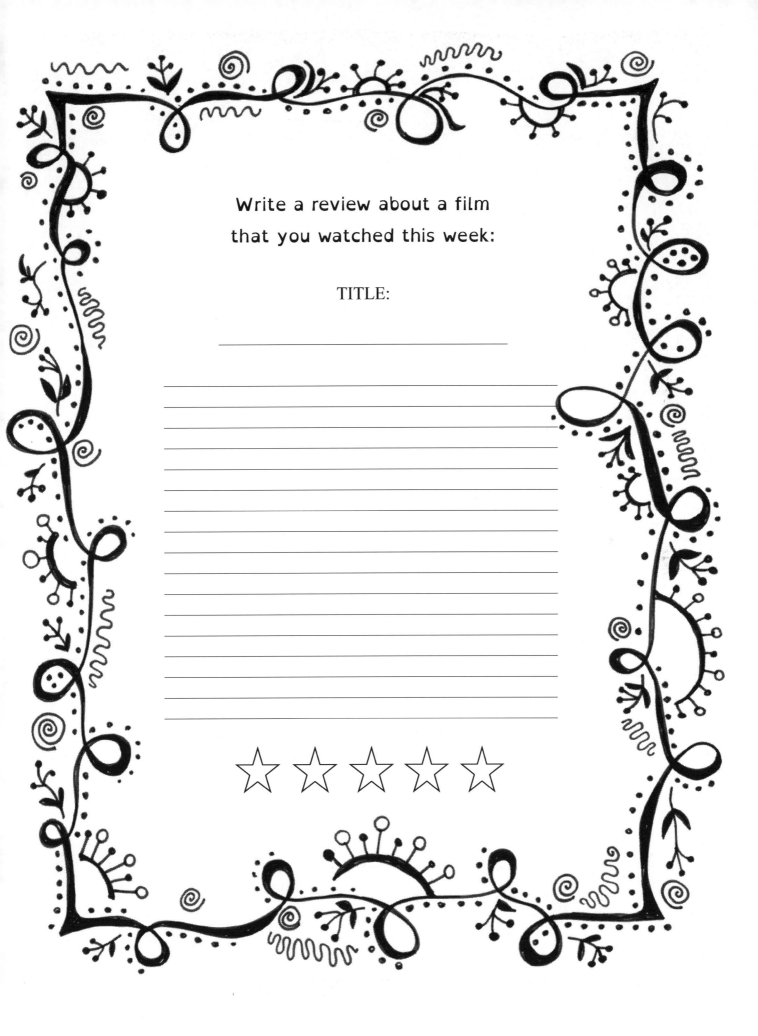

Write a review about a film
that you watched this week:

TITLE:

Draw one of your favorite scenes or characters here.

Title:_____

Draw one of your favorite scenes or characters here.

Title:_____

TITLE:_____

Today's Date:_____

Producer:

_____

Actors:

_____

_____

_____

_____

_____

_____

_____

_____

_____

_____

Rating:

AWFUL

BAD

LAME

BORING

OKAY

NICE

GOOD

GREAT

SUPER

AMAZING

Draw a Scene from the video:

Notes:

TITLE:_____

Today's Date:_____

Producer:

_____

Actors:

_____

_____

_____

_____

_____

_____

_____

_____

_____

Rating:

AWFUL

BAD

LAME

BORING

OKAY

NICE

GOOD

GREAT

SUPER

AMAZING

Draw a Scene from the video:

Notes:

TITLE:_____

Today's Date:_____

Producer:

_____

Actors:

_____

_____

_____

_____

_____

_____

_____

_____

_____

Rating:

AWFUL

BAD

LAME

BORING

OKAY

NICE

GOOD

GREAT

SUPER

AMAZING

Draw a Scene from the video:

Notes:

TITLE:_____

Today's Date:_____

Producer:

_____

Actors:

_____

_____

_____

_____

Rating:

AWFUL

BAD

LAME

BORING

OKAY

NICE

GOOD

GREAT

SUPER

AMAZING

Draw a Scene from the video:

Notes:

TITLE:_____

Today's Date:_____

Producer:

_____

Actors:

_____

_____

_____

_____

_____

_____

_____

_____

_____

_____

Rating:

AWFUL

BAD

LAME

BORING

OKAY

NICE

GOOD

GREAT

SUPER

AMAZING

Draw a Scene from the video:

Write a review about a film
that you watched this week:

TITLE:

_____

_____
_____
_____
_____
_____
_____
_____
_____
_____
_____
_____
_____
_____

☆ ☆ ☆ ☆ ☆

Draw one of your favorite scenes or characters here.

Title:_____

Draw one of your favorite scenes or characters here.

Title:_____

TITLE:_____

Today's Date:_____

Producer:

_____

Actors:

_____

_____

_____

_____

_____

_____

_____

_____

_____

Rating:

AWFUL

BAD

LAME

BORING

OKAY

NICE

GOOD

GREAT

SUPER

AMAZING

Draw a Scene from the video:

Notes:

TITLE:_____

Today's Date:_____

Producer:

_____

Actors:

_____

_____

_____

_____

_____
_____
_____
_____
_____

Rating:

AWFUL

BAD

LAME

BORING

OKAY

NICE

GOOD

GREAT

SUPER

AMAZING

Draw a Scene from the video:

Notes:

TITLE:_____

Today's Date: _____

Producer:

_____

Actors:

_____

_____

_____

_____

_____

_____

_____

_____

_____

Rating:

AWFUL

BAD

LAME

BORING

OKAY

NICE

GOOD

GREAT

SUPER

AMAZING

Draw a Scene from the video:

Notes:

Write a review about a film
that you watched this week:

TITLE:

_____

_____
_____
_____
_____
_____
_____
_____
_____
_____
_____
_____
_____
_____
_____

☆ ☆ ☆ ☆ ☆

Draw one of your favorite scenes or characters here.

Title:_____

Draw one of your favorite scenes or characters here.

Title:_____

TITLE:_____

Today's Date:_____

Producer:

_____

Actors:

_____

_____

_____

_____

_____

_____

_____

_____

_____

Rating:

AWFUL

BAD

LAME

BORING

OKAY

NICE

GOOD

GREAT

SUPER

AMAZING

Draw a Scene from the video:

Notes:

TITLE:_____

Today's Date:_____

Producer:

_____

Actors:

_____

_____

_____

_____

Rating:

AWFUL

BAD

LAME

BORING

OKAY

NICE

GOOD

GREAT

SUPER

AMAZING

Draw a Scene from the video:

Notes:

TITLE:

TITLE:_____

Today's Date:_____

Producer:

_____

Actors:

_____

_____

_____

_____

_____

_____

_____

_____

_____

Rating:

AWFUL

BAD

LAME

BORING

OKAY

NICE

GOOD

GREAT

SUPER

AMAZING

Draw a Scene from the video:

Notes:

TITLE:_____

Today's Date:_____

Producer:

_____

Actors:

_____

_____

_____

_____

_____

_____

_____

_____

_____

Rating:

AWFUL

BAD

LAME

BORING

OKAY

NICE

GOOD

GREAT

SUPER

AMAZING

Draw a Scene from the video:

Notes:

TITLE:_____

Today's Date:_____

Producer:

_____

Actors:

_____

_____

_____

_____

_____

_____

_____

_____

_____

Rating:

AWFUL

BAD

LAME

BORING

OKAY

NICE

GOOD

GREAT

SUPER

AMAZING

Draw a Scene from the video:

Notes:

Write a review about a film
that you watched this week:

TITLE:

_____

_____
_____
_____
_____
_____
_____
_____
_____
_____
_____
_____
_____
_____

☆ ☆ ☆ ☆ ☆

Draw one of your favorite scenes or characters here.

Title:_____

Draw one of your favorite scenes or characters here.

Title:_____

TITLE:_____

Today's Date:_____

Producer:

_____

Actors:

_____

_____

_____

_____

_____
_____
_____
_____
_____

Rating:
AWFUL
BAD
LAME
BORING
OKAY
NICE
GOOD
GREAT
SUPER
AMAZING

Draw a Scene from the video:

Notes:

TITLE:_____

Today's Date:_____

Producer:

_____

Actors:

_____

_____

_____

_____

_____
_____
_____
_____
_____

Rating:
AWFUL
BAD
LAME
BORING
OKAY
NICE
GOOD
GREAT
SUPER
AMAZING

Draw a Scene from the video:

Notes:

TITLE:

TITLE:_____

Today's Date:_____

Producer:

_____

Actors:

_____

_____

_____

_____

_____
_____
_____
_____
_____

Rating:

AWFUL

BAD

LAME

BORING

OKAY

NICE

GOOD

GREAT

SUPER

AMAZING

Draw a Scene from the video:

Notes:

Write a review about a film
that you watched this week:

TITLE:

_____

_____
_____
_____
_____
_____
_____
_____
_____
_____
_____
_____
_____
_____
_____

☆ ☆ ☆ ☆ ☆

TITLE:_____

Today's Date:_____

Producer:

_____

Actors:

_____

_____

_____

_____

_____

_____

_____

_____

_____

Rating:

AWFUL

BAD

LAME

BORING

OKAY

NICE

GOOD

GREAT

SUPER

AMAZING

Draw a Scene from the video:

Notes:

TITLE:_____

Today's Date:_____

Producer:

_____

Actors:

_____

_____

_____

_____

Rating:

AWFUL

BAD

LAME

BORING

OKAY

NICE

GOOD

GREAT

SUPER

AMAZING

Draw a Scene from the video:

Notes:

Draw one of your favorite scenes or characters here.

Title:_____

Draw one of your favorite scenes or characters here.

Title:_____

TITLE:_____

Today's Date:_____

Producer:

_____

Actors:

_____

_____

_____

_____

_____
_____
_____
_____
_____

Rating:

AWFUL

BAD

LAME

BORING

OKAY

NICE

GOOD

GREAT

SUPER

AMAZING

Draw a Scene from the video:

Notes:

Write a review about a film
that you watched this week:

TITLE:

_____

_____
_____
_____
_____
_____
_____
_____
_____
_____
_____
_____
_____
_____
_____

☆ ☆ ☆ ☆ ☆

TITLE:_____

Today's Date:_____

Producer:

_____

Actors:

_____

_____

_____

_____

_____

_____

_____

_____

_____

Rating:

AWFUL

BAD

LAME

BORING

OKAY

NICE

GOOD

GREAT

SUPER

AMAZING

Draw a Scene from the video:

Notes:

TITLE:_____

Today's Date:_____

Producer:

_____

Actors:

_____

_____

_____

_____

_____
_____
_____
_____
_____
_____

Rating:

AWFUL

BAD

LAME

BORING

OKAY

NICE

GOOD

GREAT

SUPER

AMAZING

Draw a Scene from the video:

Notes:

TITLE:_____

Today's Date:_____

Producer:

_____

Actors:

_____

_____

_____

_____

_____

_____

_____

_____

_____

Rating:

AWFUL

BAD

LAME

BORING

OKAY

NICE

GOOD

GREAT

SUPER

AMAZING

Draw a Scene from the video:

Notes:

Write a review about a film
that you watched this week:

TITLE:

_____

_____
_____
_____
_____
_____
_____
_____
_____
_____
_____
_____
_____
_____
_____

☆ ☆ ☆ ☆ ☆

Draw one of your favorite scenes or characters here.

Title:_____

Draw one of your favorite scenes or characters here.

Title:_____

TITLE:_____

Today's Date:_____

Producer:

_____

Actors:

_____

_____

_____

_____

_____
_____
_____
_____
_____

Rating:

AWFUL

BAD

LAME

BORING

OKAY

NICE

GOOD

GREAT

SUPER

AMAZING

Draw a Scene from the video:

Notes:

TITLE:_____

Today's Date:_____

Producer:

_____

Actors:

_____

_____

_____

_____

_____
_____
_____
_____
_____

Rating:

AWFUL

BAD

LAME

BORING

OKAY

NICE

GOOD

GREAT

SUPER

AMAZING

Draw a Scene from the video:

Notes:

TITLE:_____

Today's Date:_____

Producer:

_____

Actors:

_____

_____

_____

_____

_____

_____

_____

_____

_____

_____

Rating:

AWFUL

BAD

LAME

BORING

OKAY

NICE

GOOD

GREAT

SUPER

AMAZING

Draw a Scene from the video:

Notes:

TITLE:_____

Today's Date:_____

Producer:

_____

Actors:

_____

_____

_____

_____

_____

_____

_____

_____

_____

Rating:

AWFUL

BAD

LAME

BORING

OKAY

NICE

GOOD

GREAT

SUPER

AMAZING

Draw a Scene from the video:

Notes:

TITLE:_____

Today's Date:_____

Producer:

_____

Actors:

_____

_____

_____

_____

_____

_____

_____

_____

_____

Rating:

AWFUL

BAD

LAME

BORING

OKAY

NICE

GOOD

GREAT

SUPER

AMAZING

Draw a Scene from the video:

Notes:

Write a review about a film
that you watched this week:

TITLE:

_____

_____
_____
_____
_____
_____
_____
_____
_____
_____
_____
_____
_____

☆ ☆ ☆ ☆ ☆

Draw one of your favorite scenes or characters here.

Title:_____

Draw one of your favorite scenes or characters here.

Title:_____

TITLE:_____

Today's Date:_____

Producer:

_____

Actors:

_____

_____

_____

_____

_____

_____

_____

_____

_____

_____

Rating:

AWFUL

BAD

LAME

BORING

OKAY

NICE

GOOD

GREAT

SUPER

AMAZING

Draw a Scene from the video:

Notes:

TITLE:_____

Today's Date:_____

Producer:

_____

Actors:

_____

_____

_____

_____

_____

_____

_____

_____

_____

Rating:

AWFUL

BAD

LAME

BORING

OKAY

NICE

GOOD

GREAT

SUPER

AMAZING

Draw a Scene from the video:

Notes:

TITLE:_____

Today's Date:_____

Producer:

_____

Actors:

_____

_____

_____

_____

- - - - - - - - - - - - - - - - - -

- - - - - - - - - - - - - - - - - -

- - - - - - - - - - - - - - - - - -

- - - - - - - - - - - - - - - - - -

- - - - - - - - - - - - - - - - - -

Rating:

AWFUL

BAD

LAME

BORING

OKAY

NICE

GOOD

GREAT

SUPER

AMAZING

Draw a Scene from the video:

Notes:

TITLE:_____

Today's Date:_____

Producer:

_____

Actors:

_____

_____

_____

_____

_____
_____
_____
_____
_____

Rating:

AWFUL

BAD

LAME

BORING

OKAY

NICE

GOOD

GREAT

SUPER

AMAZING

Draw a Scene from the video:

Notes:

TITLE:_____

Today's Date:_____

Producer:

Actors:

Rating:

AWFUL

BAD

LAME

BORING

OKAY

NICE

GOOD

GREAT

SUPER

AMAZING

Draw a Scene from the video:

Notes:

Write a review about a film
that you watched this week:

TITLE:

_____

_____
_____
_____
_____
_____
_____
_____
_____
_____
_____
_____

☆ ☆ ☆ ☆ ☆

Draw one of your favorite scenes or characters here.

Title:_____

Draw one of your favorite scenes or characters here.

Title:_____

TITLE:_____

Today's Date:_____

Producer:

_____

Actors:

_____

_____

_____

_____

_____

_____

_____

_____

_____

Rating:

AWFUL

BAD

LAME

BORING

OKAY

NICE

GOOD

GREAT

SUPER

AMAZING

Draw a Scene from the video:

Notes:

TITLE:_____

Today's Date:_____

Producer:

_____

Actors:

_____

_____

_____

_____

_____
_____
_____
_____
_____

Rating:

AWFUL

BAD

LAME

BORING

OKAY

NICE

GOOD

GREAT

SUPER

AMAZING

Draw a Scene from the video:

Notes:

TITLE:_____

Today's Date:_____

Producer:

_____

Actors:

_____

_____

_____

_____

_____

_____

_____

_____

_____

Rating:

AWFUL

BAD

LAME

BORING

OKAY

NICE

GOOD

GREAT

SUPER

AMAZING

Draw a Scene from the video:

Notes:

Write a review about a film
that you watched this week:

TITLE:

_____

_____
_____
_____
_____
_____
_____
_____
_____
_____
_____
_____
_____
_____
_____

☆ ☆ ☆ ☆ ☆

Draw one of your favorite scenes or characters here.

Title:_____

Draw one of your favorite scenes or characters here.

Title:_____

Draw one of your favorite scenes or characters here.

Title:_____

Draw one of your favorite scenes or characters here.

Title:_____

Draw one of your favorite scenes or characters here.

Title:_____

Do It Yourself
HOMESCHOOL
RESOURCES

Copyright Information

Contact Us:
The Thinking Tree LLC
Jbrown@DyslexiaGames.com
www.FunSchoolingBooks.com